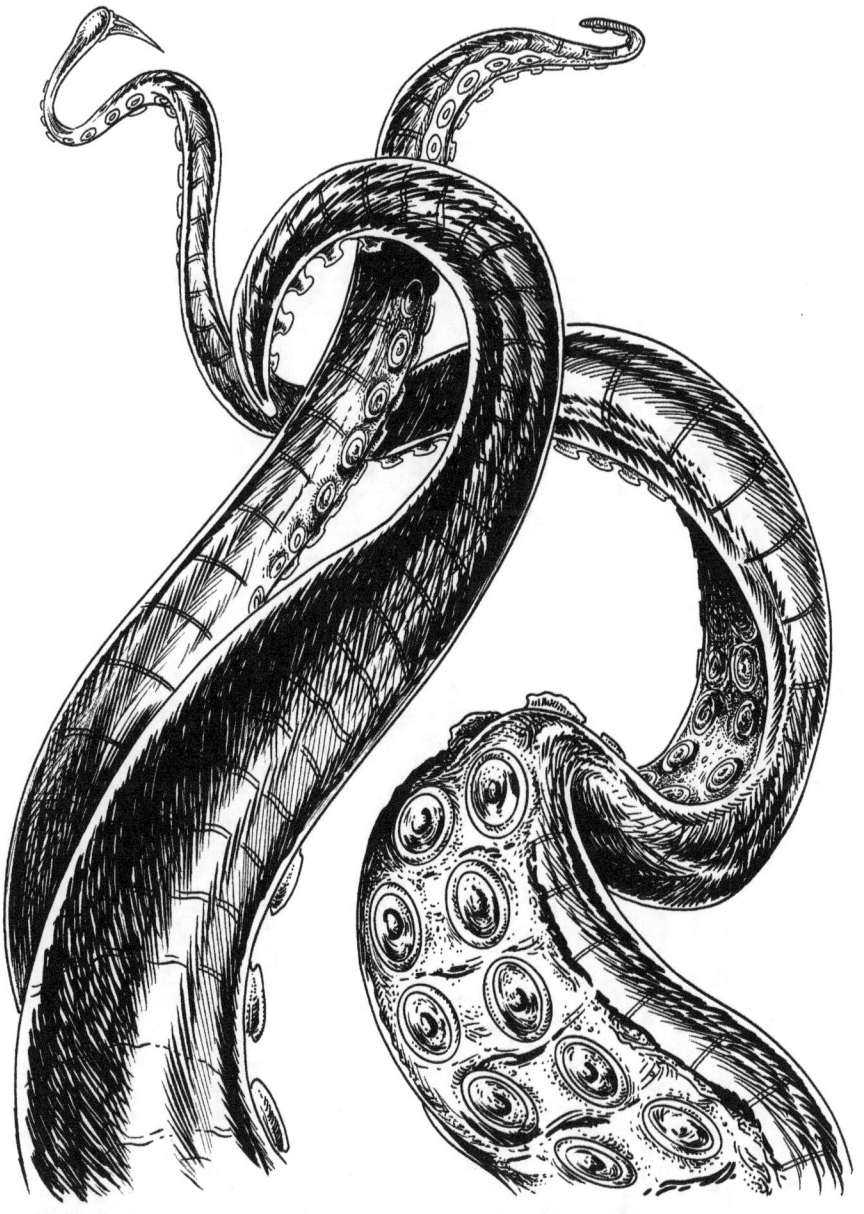

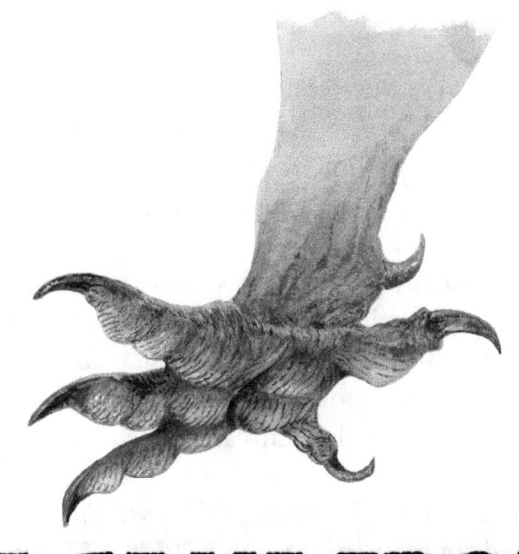

IT CAME FROM THE MIST

The Mist
Art
By Glenn Chadbourne

Inspired by the fiction of Stephen King's
original novella, *The Mist*.

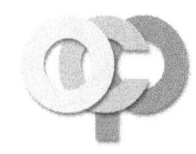

OVERLOOK CONNECTION PRESS

2019

To the fine fellows who brought the creatures out of...

...The Mist.

Stephen King

Frank Darabont

Berni Wrightson

Glenn Chadbourne

Vatskizzle

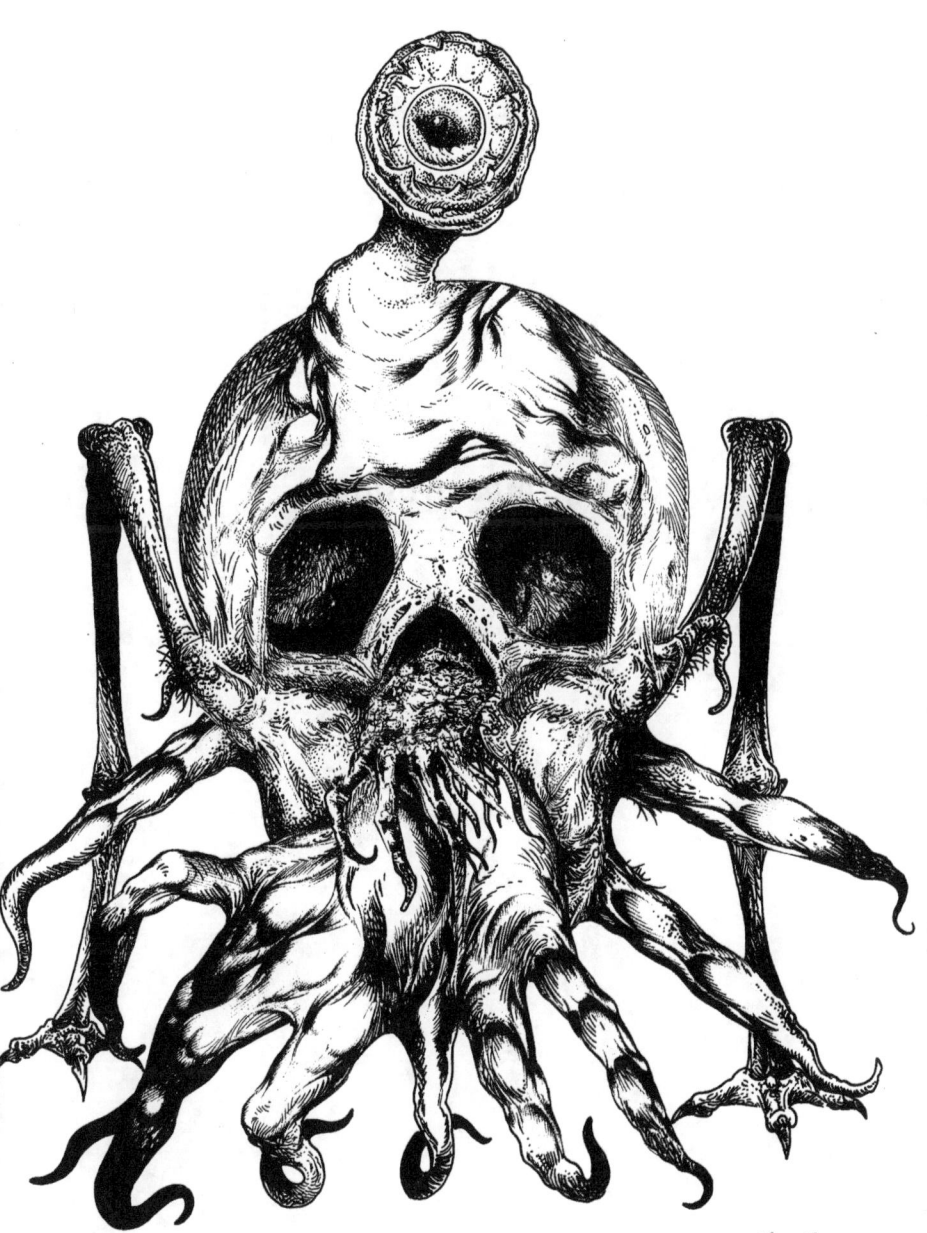

Yoincalvosum

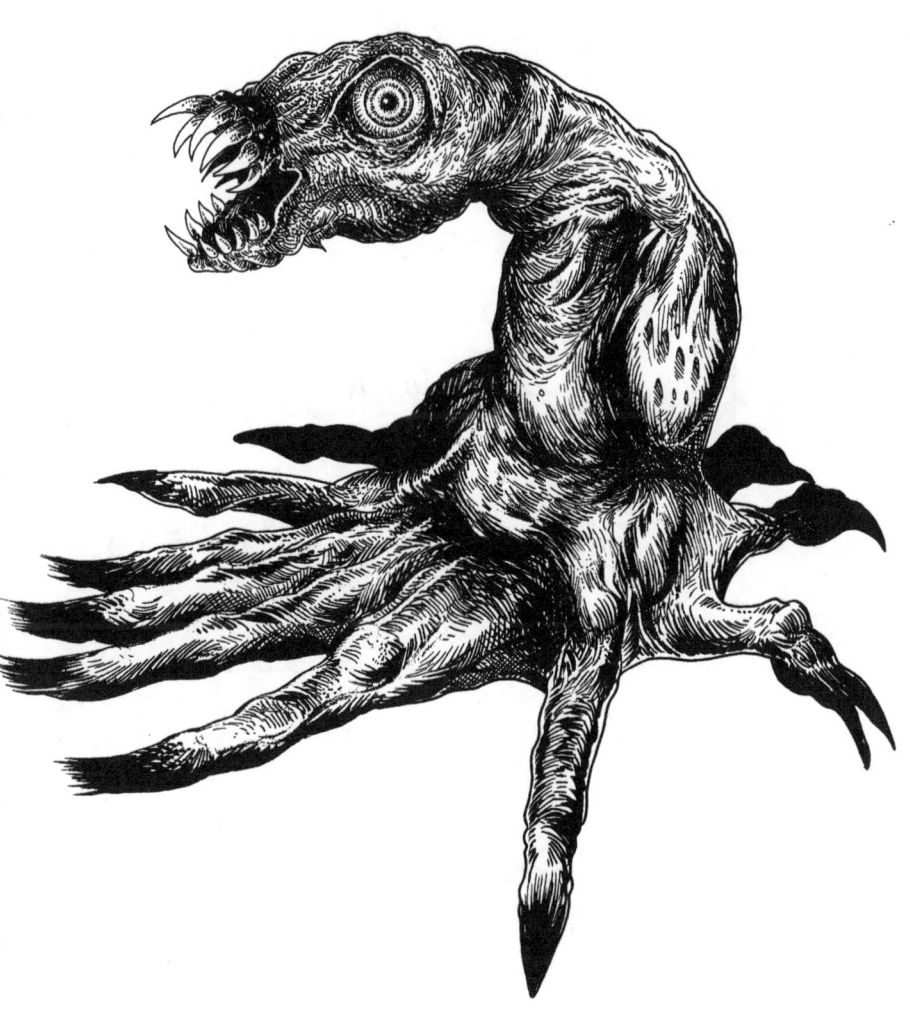

CHADBOURNE 2018—

Beekitdozzle

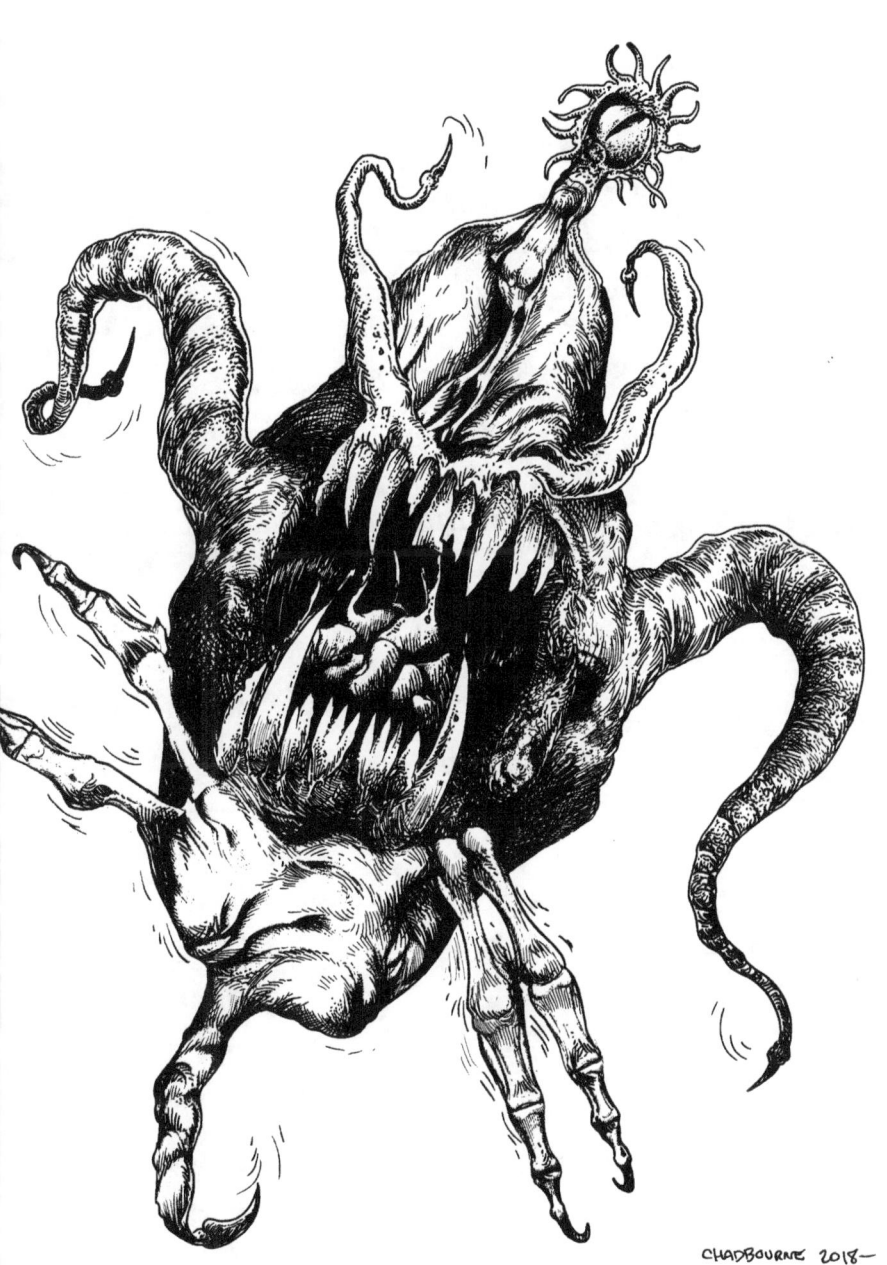

CHADBOURNE 2018—

Yamakep

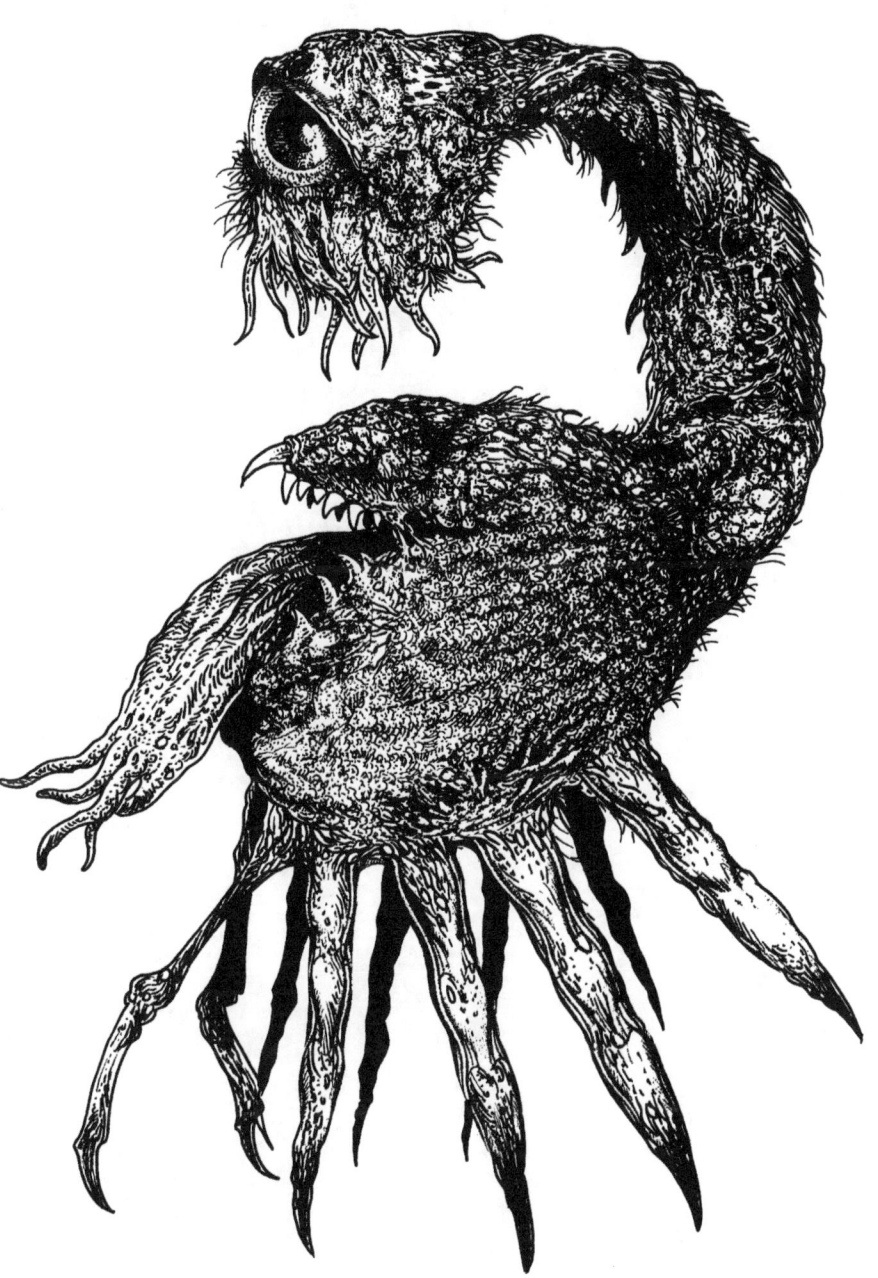

CHADBOURNE 2015

Horned Poontuttle

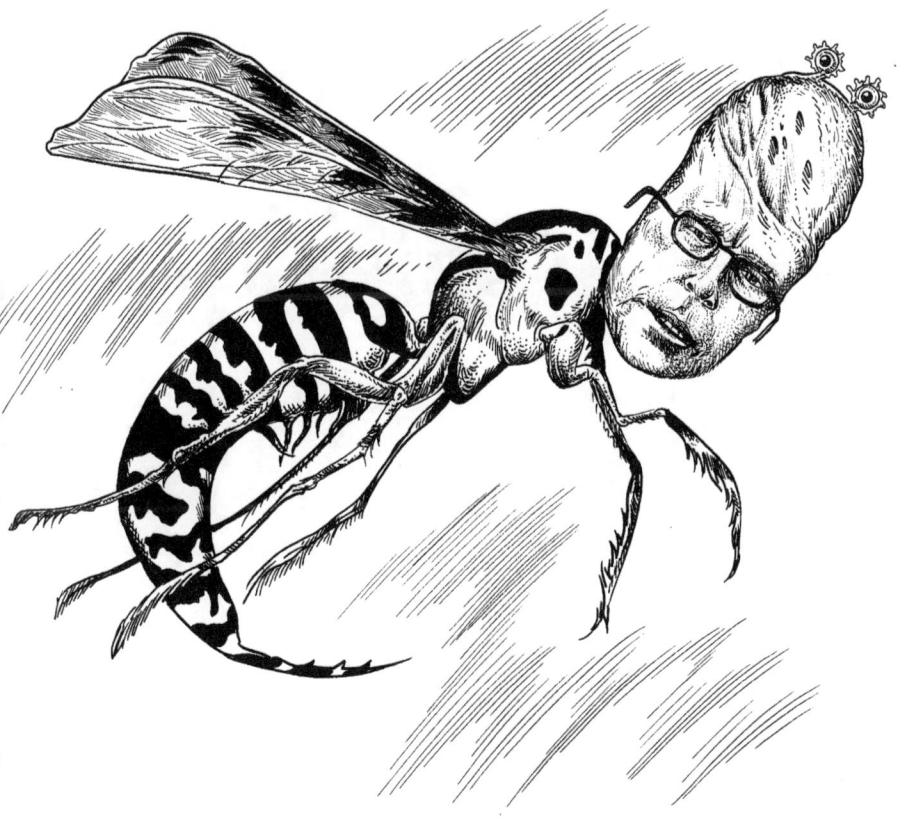

CHADBOURNE 2018—

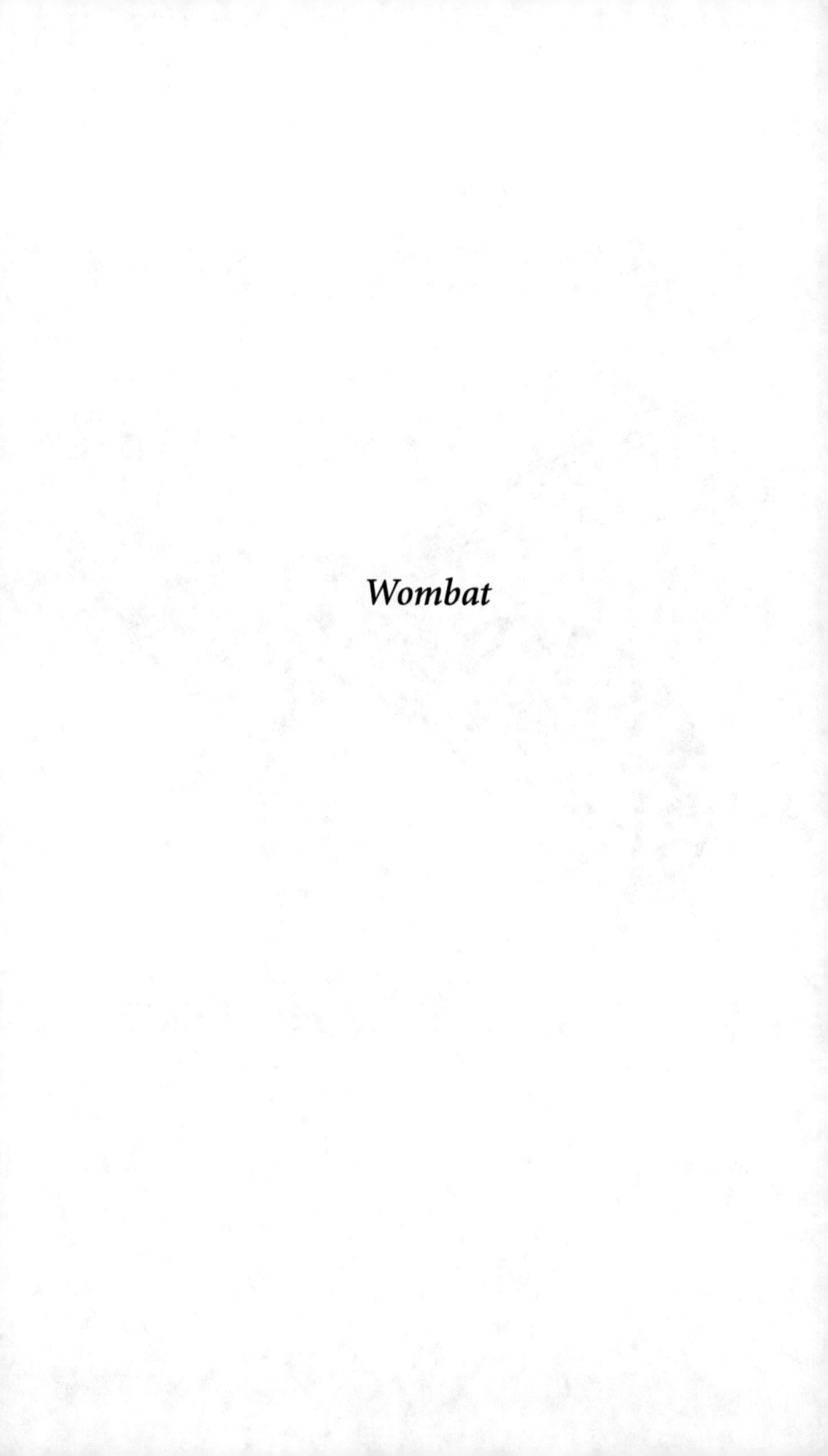

Wombat

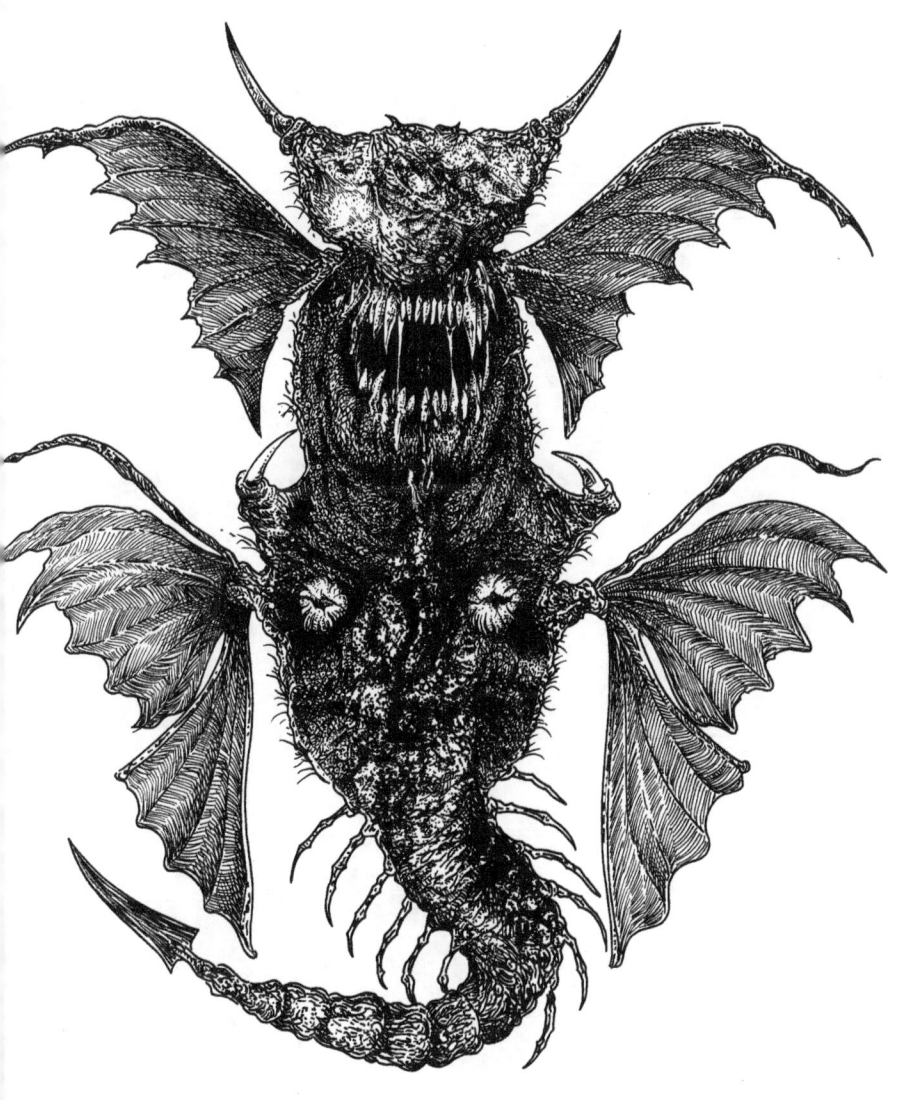

CHADBOURNE 2018

Zyfoodle

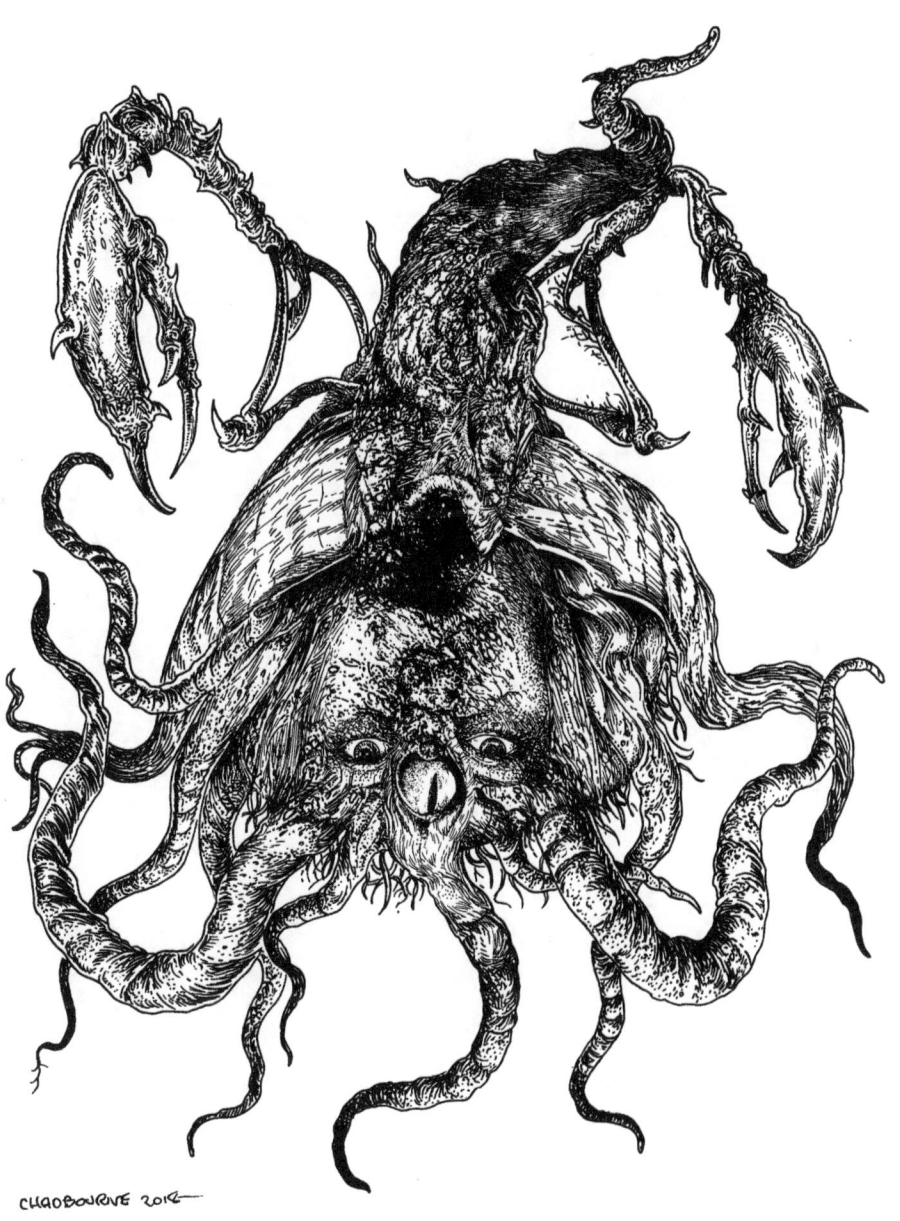

CHADBOURNE 2012

Inkaposta

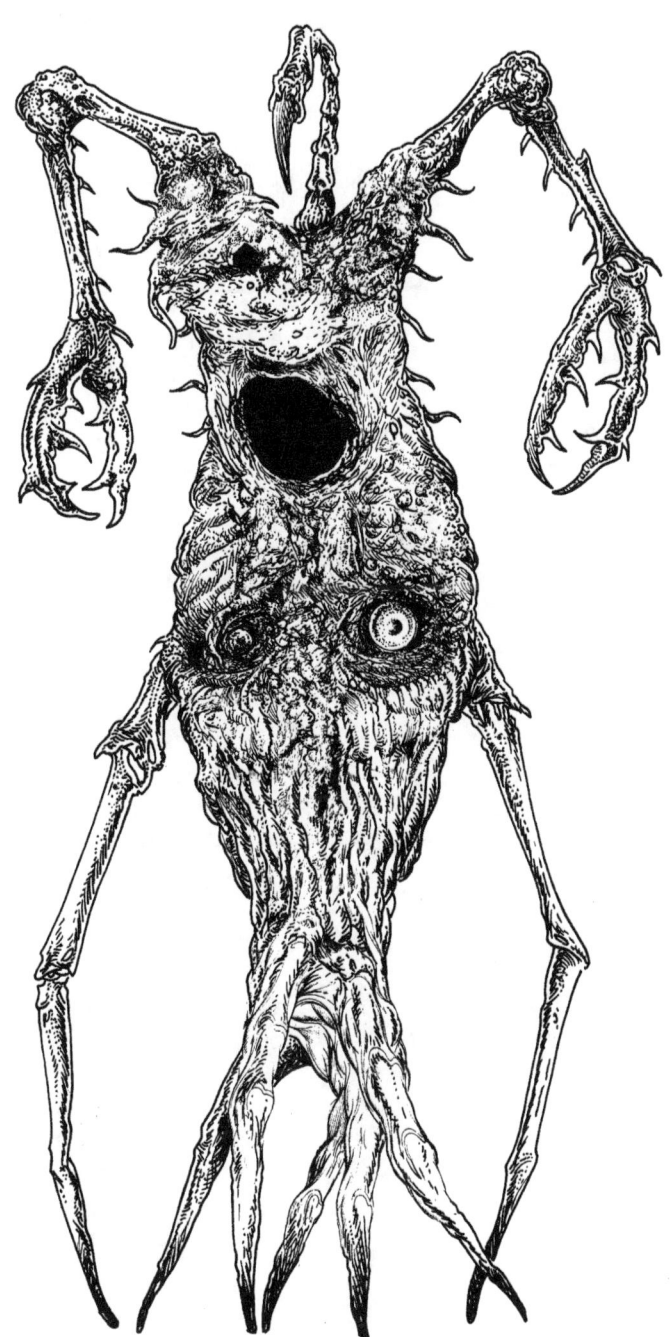

CHADBOURNE 2018—

Boontunny

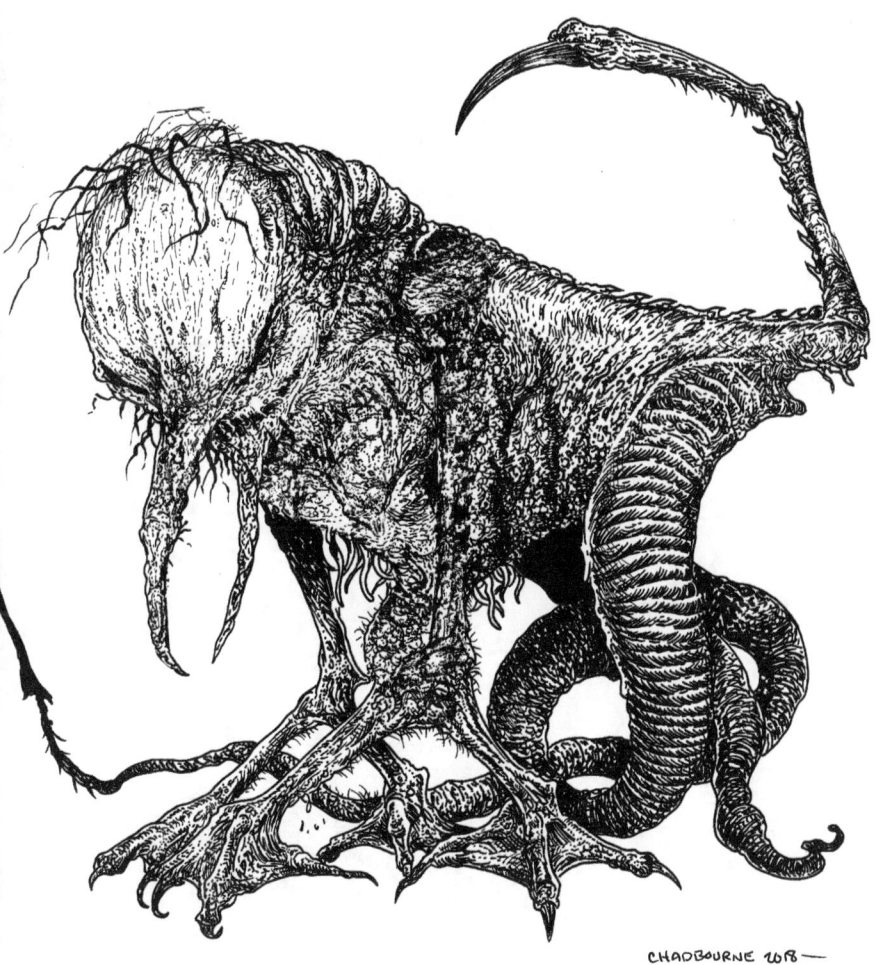

CHADBOURNE 2018

Rodskink

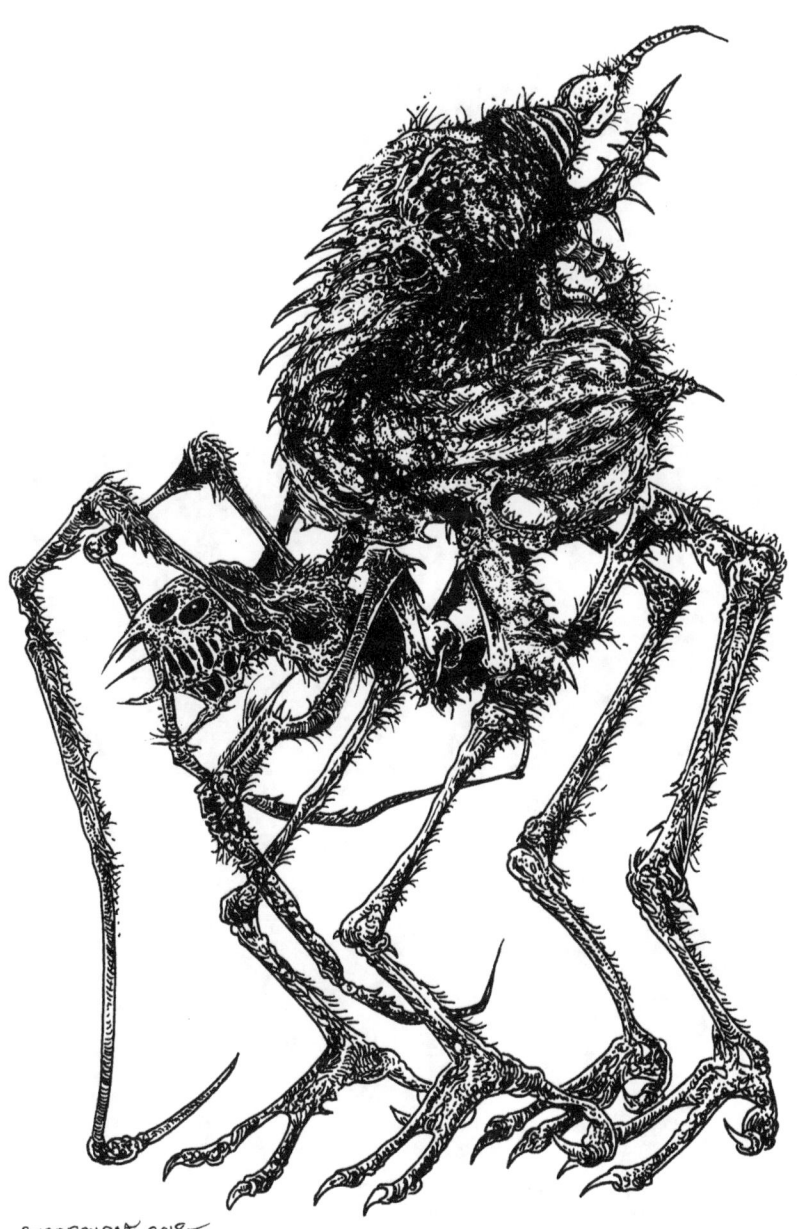

CHADBOURNE 2018

Vordalacundrea

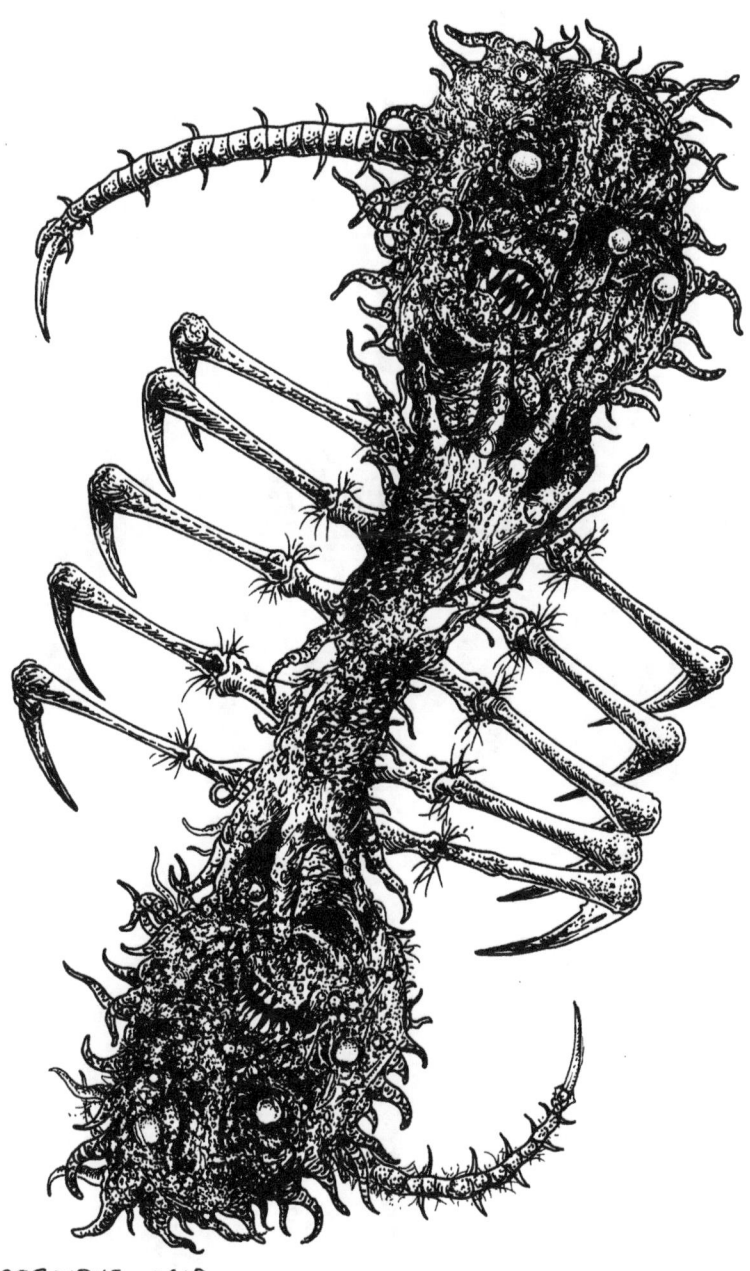

CHADBOURNE - 2018

Quimtinnie

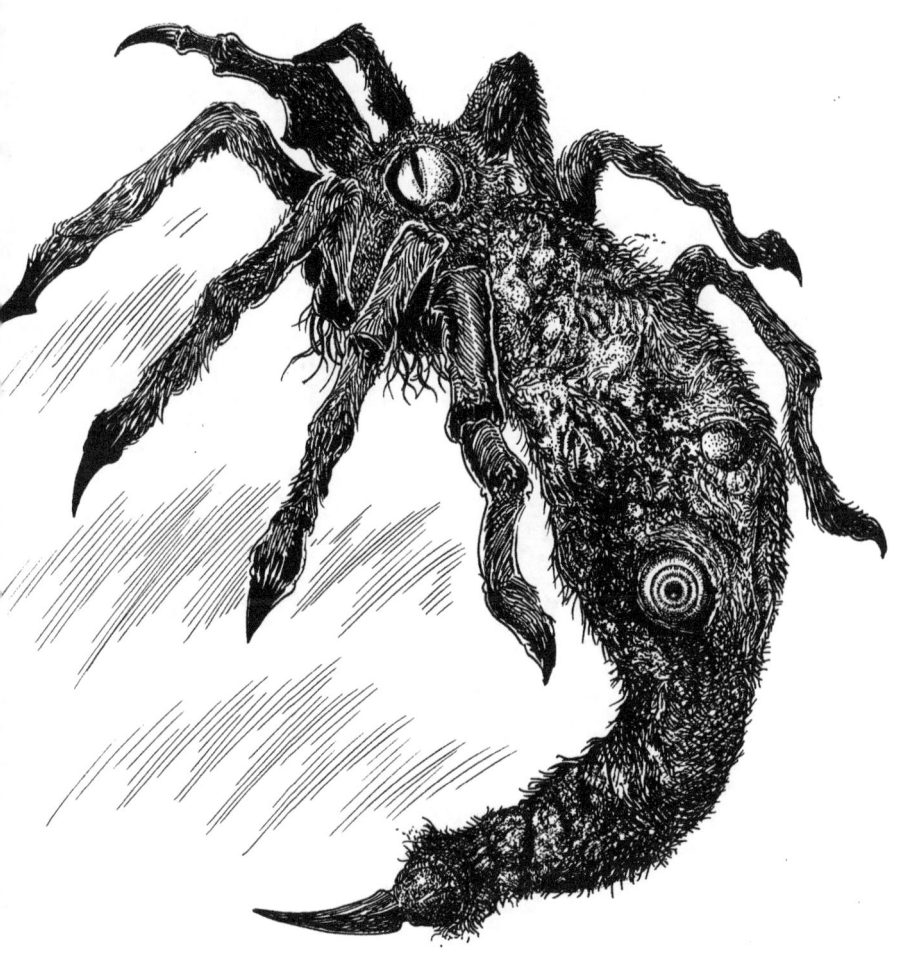

CHADBOURNE 2018 —

Tinner Ziskafoont

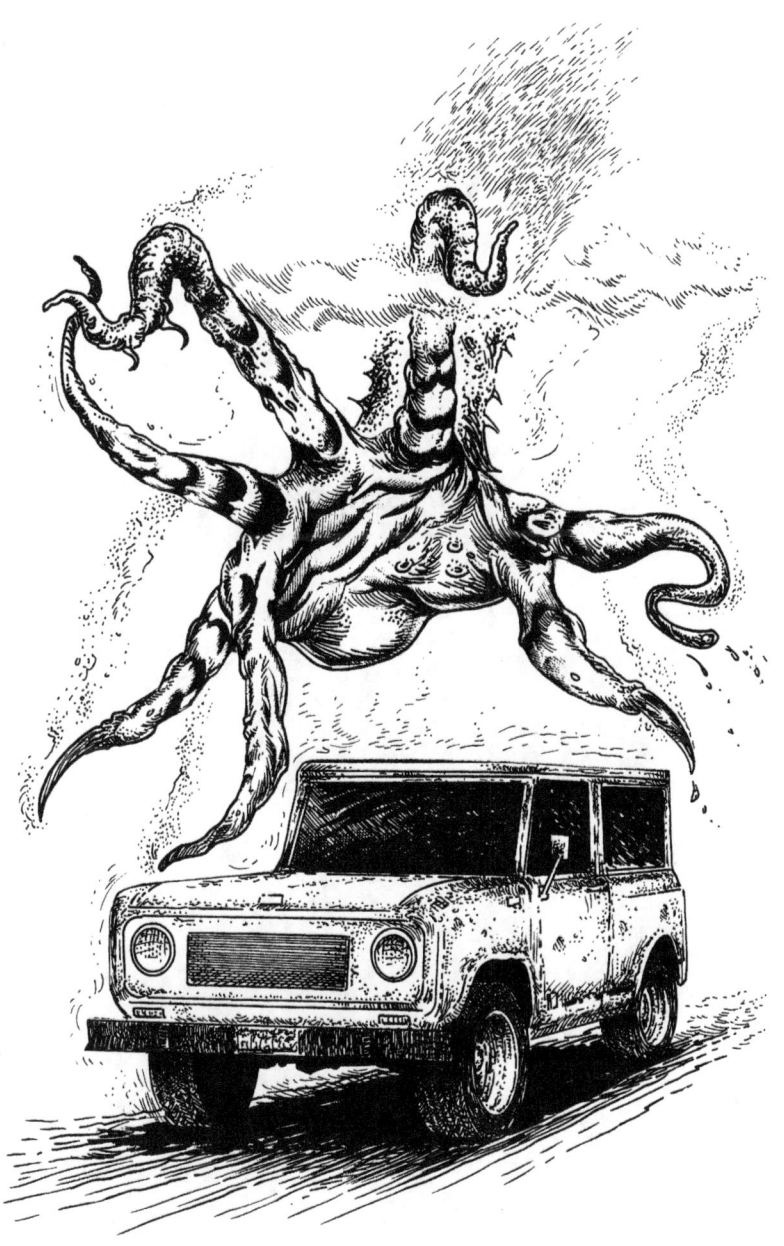

CHADBOURNE 2018

Barnscuppet

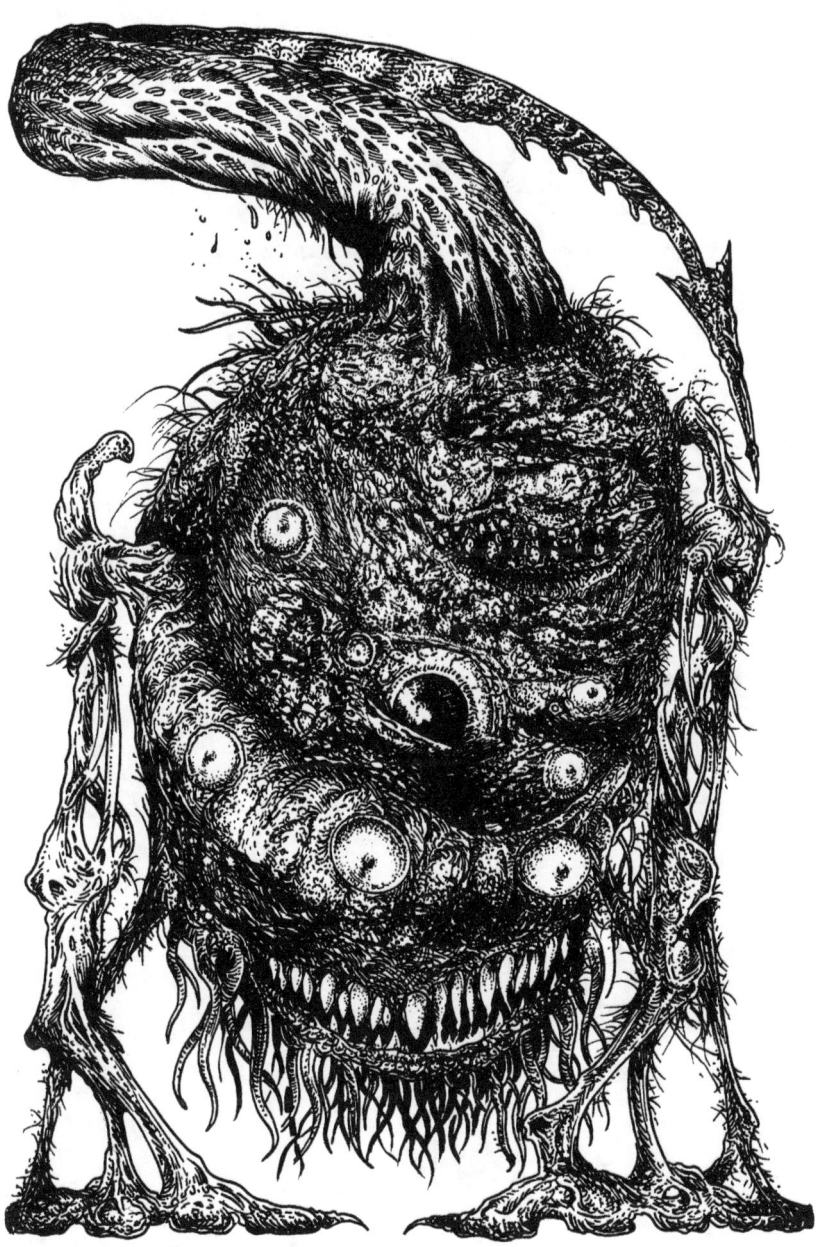

CHADBOURNE 2018

Zubatski

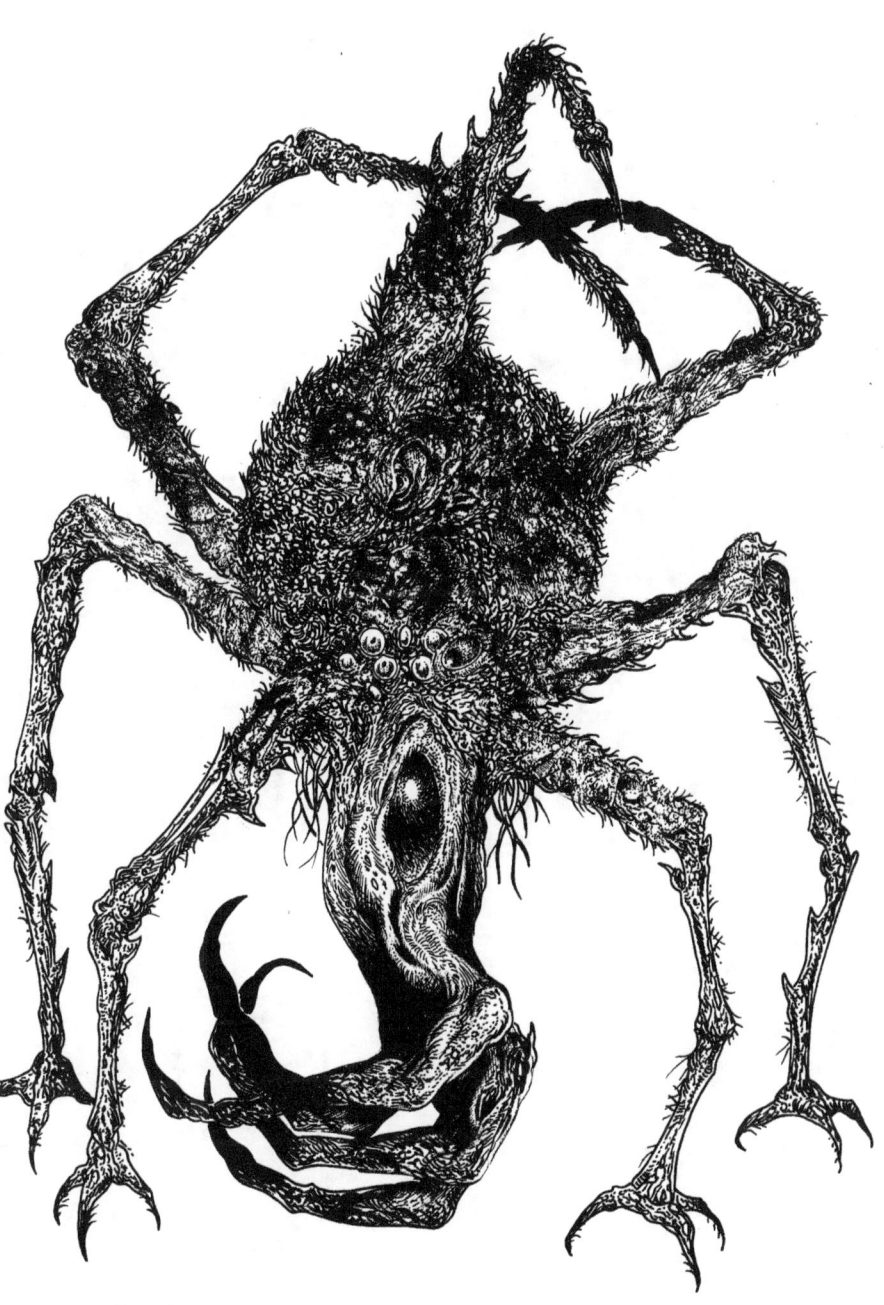

CHADBOURNE 2018—

Dondlefrut

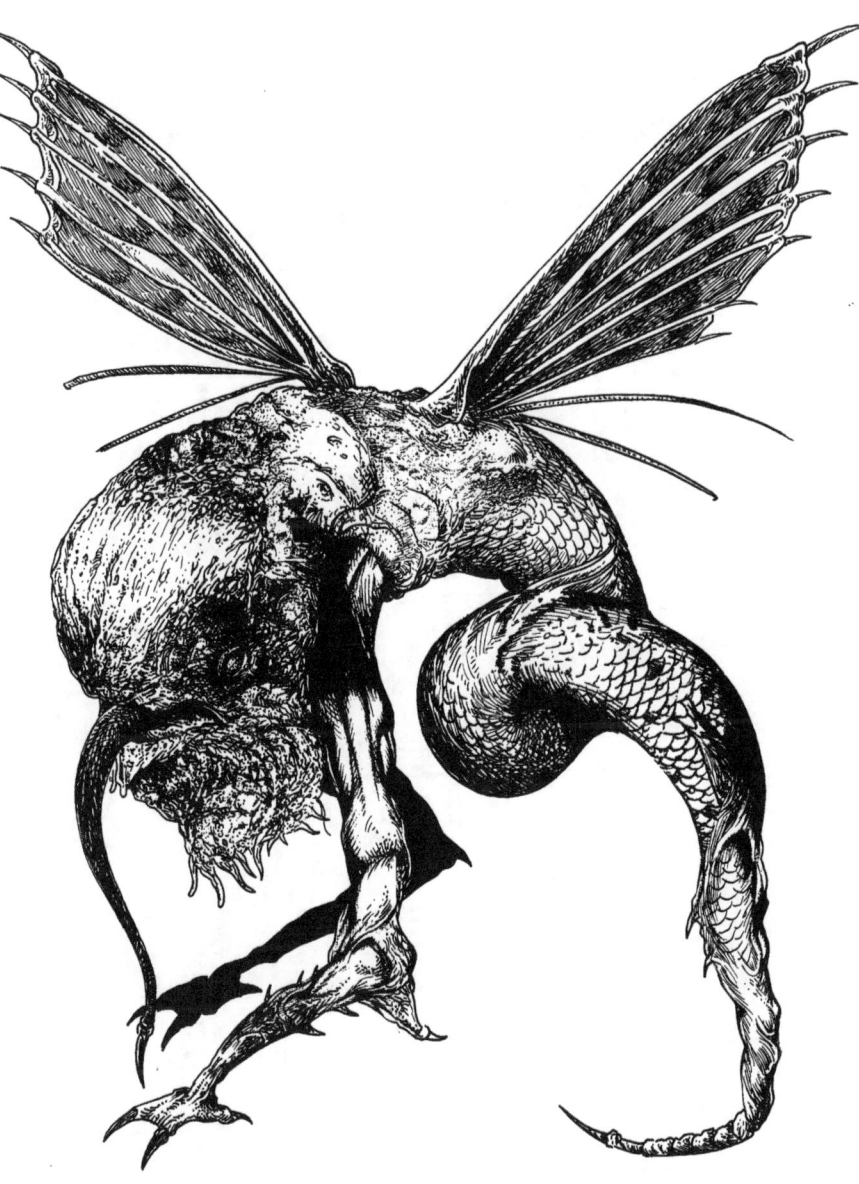

CHADROURIVE 2018

Poontango

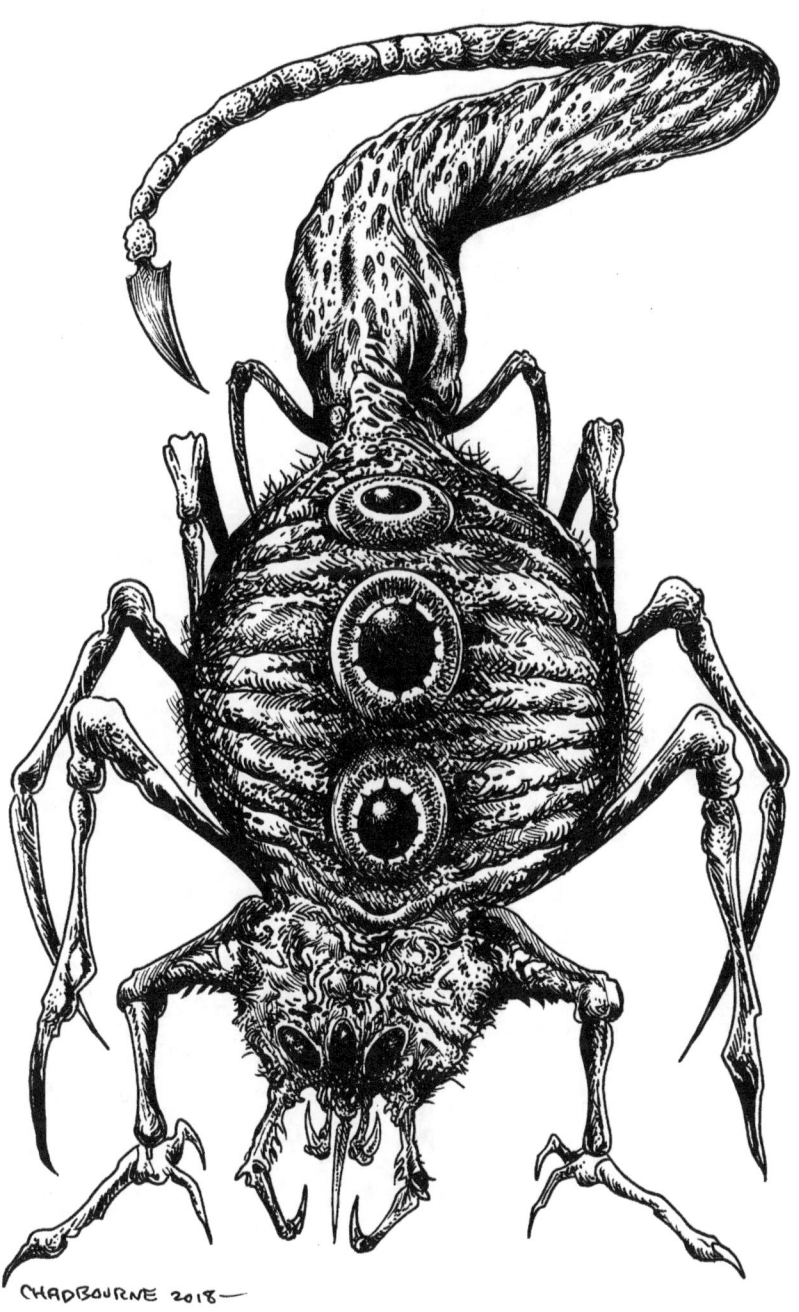

CHADBOURNE 2018

Teenywumbit

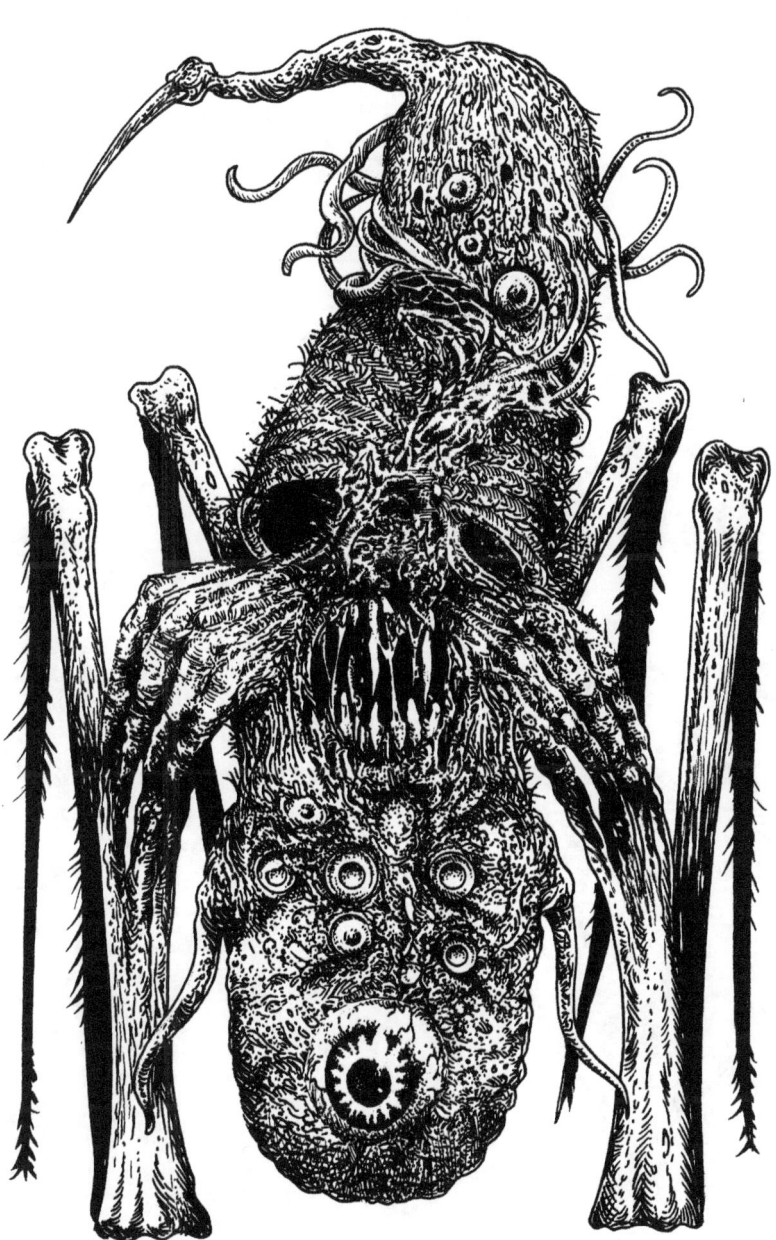

CHADBOURNE 2018—

Teet-tick

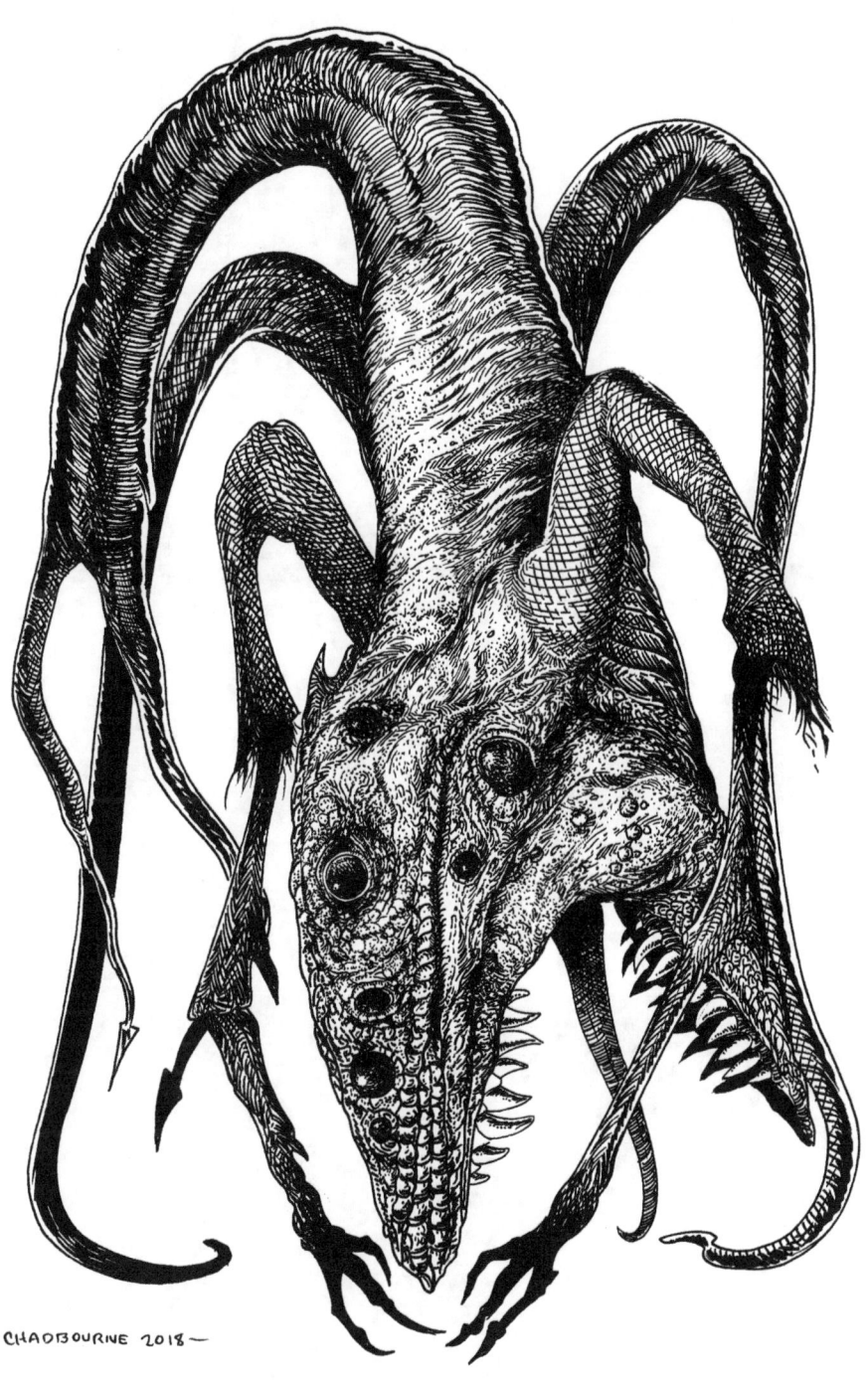

CHADBOURNE 2018

Wangsnuffet

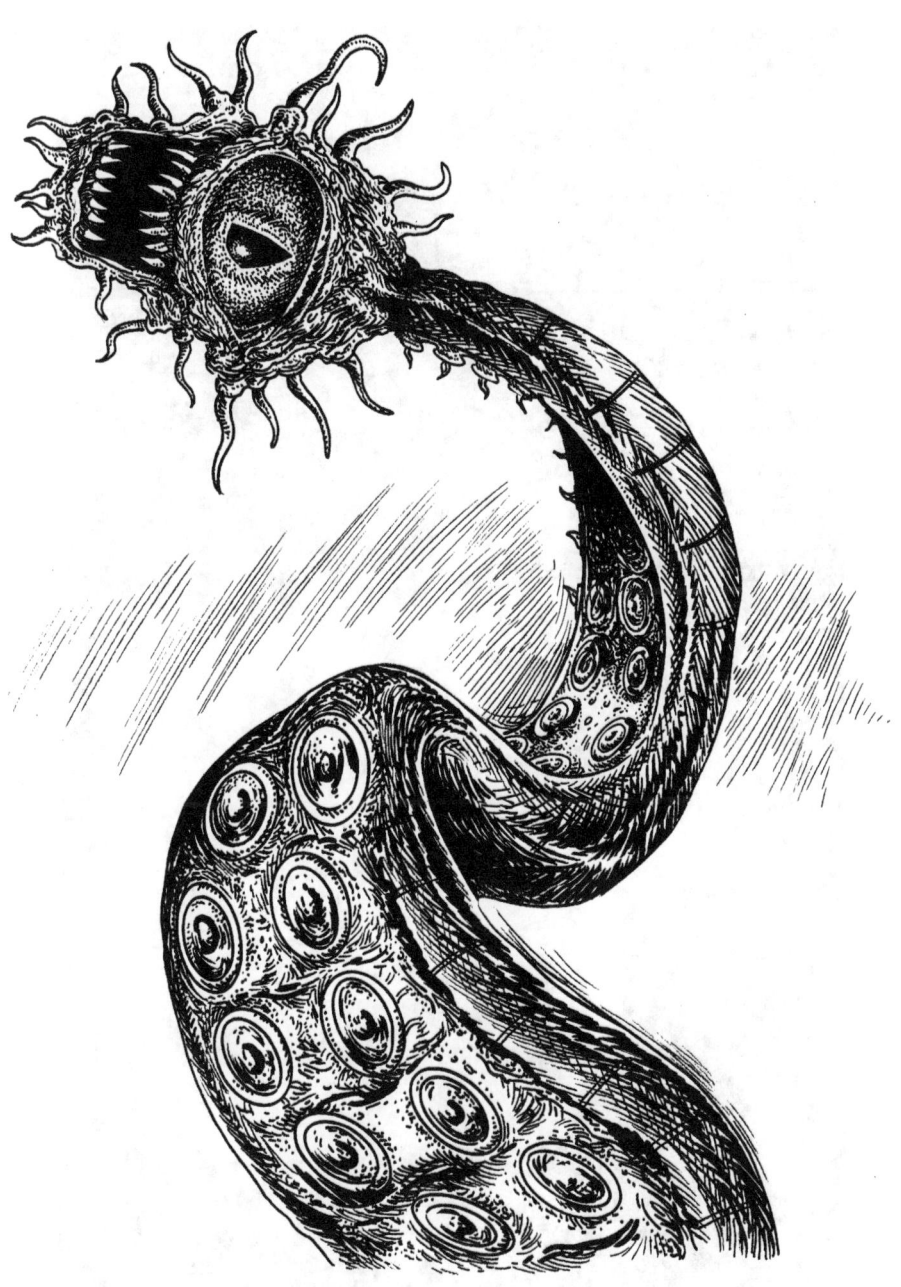

CHADBOURNE 2018—

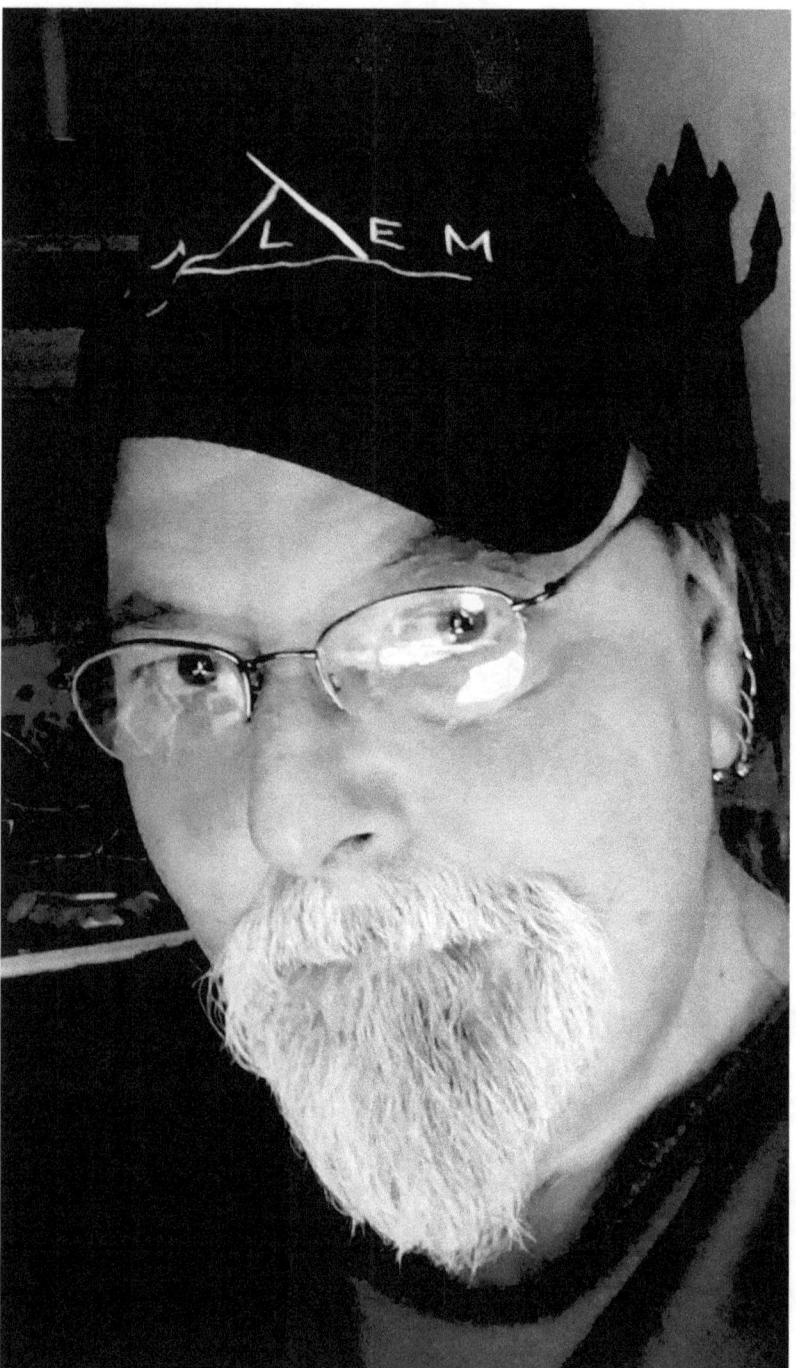

About Glenn Chadbourne

This collection of drawings are inspired by Stephen King's novella, *THE MIST*, and recently created when *THE MIST* novel was released in a new version in 2018. Thus was born this collection of original artwork, *IT CAME FROM THE MIST*.

Glenn Chadbourne is well known in the horror world of writers, artists, and even in film (if you look close in Stephen King's film, *THE MIST*, directed by Frank Darabont, you'll see Glenn's work make a cameo appearance). Artist to the stars, we all call him. Illustrator of so many novels and short story collections, including Joe Lansdale, Douglas Clegg, Rick Hautala, and especially, Stephen King special editions. Too many to mention here, but he did create a beautiful two-volume oversized illustrated set, *THE SECRETARY OF DREAMS*, a short story collection that spans some of Stephen King's best short fiction, published by Cemetery Dance Publications. In 2016 Glenn Chadbourne released *UNCLE GLENNY'S ZOMBIE 'POCALYPSE: AN ADULT COLORING BOOK*. Based on concepts he co-created with OCP publisher, Dave Hinchberger, you can see and feel in these panels that horror and humor are truly part of a double-edged sword. If you ever get a chance to meet ol' "Uncle Glenny," be sure to bring up some of the horror you've enjoyed in your life travels. Especially film, he loves a good, juicy, story, but don't hold back the gore... he wants to hear about every visceral, morsel. You never know, you're description may end up in a future drawing!

Glenn frequently visits a beach near his home in Maine, a place he calls, "Pumpkin Cove." This little out of sight area is a beach with lots of rocks, not sand mind you, and thick, shadowy, forests that hang to the left and right of this dark water bay. You wouldn't want to be caught alone there at night, but you do get a feel of the world that Glenn Chadbourne belongs too and where he dredges up these ideas to insert in the stories he illustrates. No, you wouldn't want to be out at the "cove" at night.

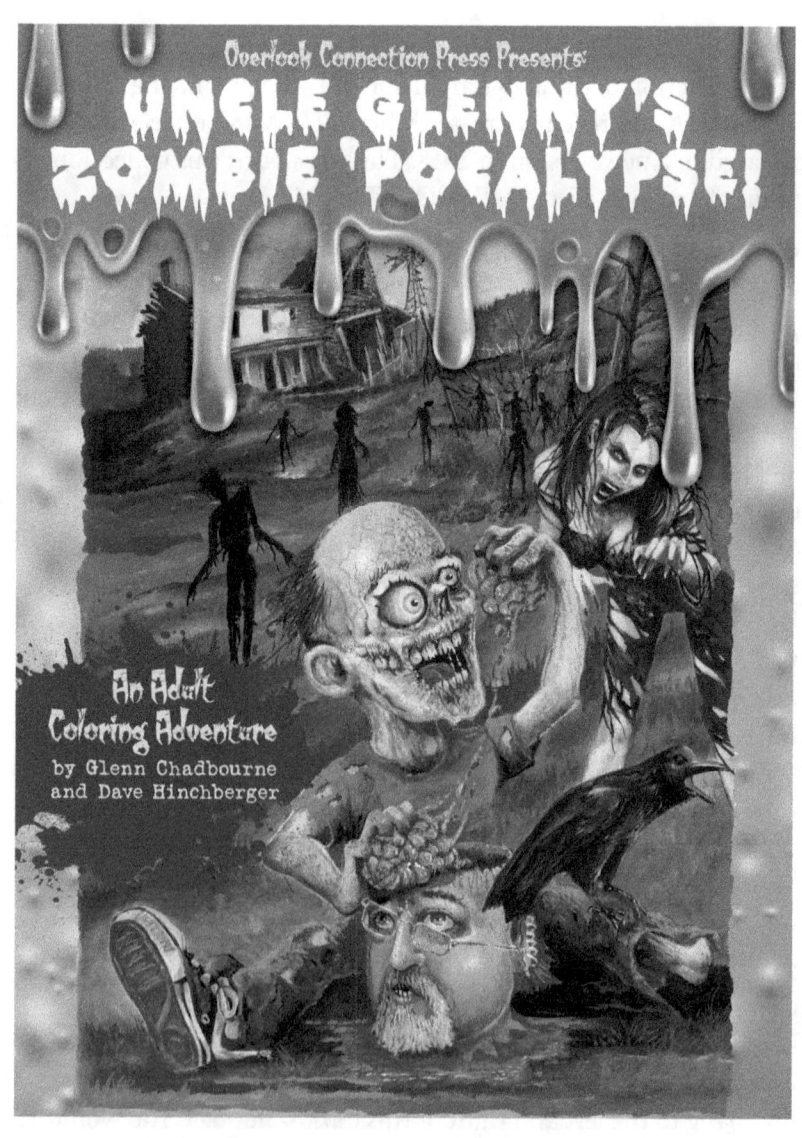

About Dave Hinchberger, Publisher of Overlook Connection Press

I devour everything. Whether its movies or comic books, novels or theater, Rock n' Roll to Jazz. Ever hear "Blue Belle Knoll," by the Cocteau Twins? I can't understand a word they're saying, it's not in my tongue of English, but the passion in this dark and beautiful piece speaks volumes to me. If it sounds good, I like it. I have so many interests that my niece calls me, "Mr. Entertainment." More so because I wanted to share the great, cool, stories I find in any medium. My family didn't always appreciate what I brought to them (*Dawn of the Dead* was too much for some), but they did enjoy the variety. Horror and Stephen King grabbed me by the boo-boo when I was knee high to the teen age. I think where it all really began was listening to the *CBS Mystery Theater* stories, on the car radio, late at night with my family on long car trips. All of my brothers, and sister, huddled in behind mom and dad in the station wagon, as the fateful sound of the drum roll theme, came echoing out of the tinny car speakers. I also think it was watching *PLANET OF THE APES* in the theater with my dad, at the age of 6, that really showed me what horror could have in store for us. Funny enough, it also intrigued me. At 10 I stumbled upon Jack Kirby's *KAMANDI: The Last Boy on Earth*. He really impressed this young man, living off a dirt road in the wilds of southern Georgia.

Since then I had thoroughly became immersed in the world of Rock n' Roll. I've managed record stores, worked a decade for Polygram Records (a helluva education), and became a publisher in my own right, as you can attest with the book you now hold in your hands. I also manage The Overlook Connection Bookstore, and its brother in horror, Stephen King Catalog, since 1987. There's so much to see, read, and experience, and these days I get to share it with my lovely wife, LeeAnn, and our sons Johnathan, Clay, Ian, Kyle, and Trey. Trey, who has his own moniker for the walking dead: "Zambies." We're nestled in a suburb of Atlanta, Georgia, where I continue to spread the good word, and art, in the world of the fantastic.

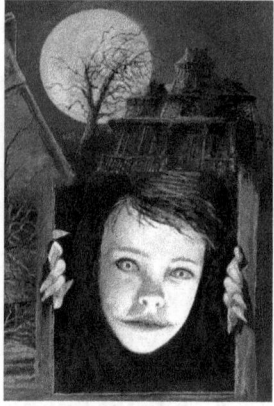

The New Stephen King Cover Series!

A *NEW* COVER FOR *EVERY* STEPHEN KING BOOK!

The New Stephen King Cover Series is an ongoing project of original paintings based on all Stephen King novels and collections. These original dust jacket covers are signed limited edition wraparound cover art, by acclaimed Stephen King artist, Glenn Chadbourne.

– *Start Your Collection, TODAY!* –

Each feature a guest author, or original art, on the dust jacket flaps.

Covers / Guest Authors

1. **The Shining**
2. **Doctor Sleep**
   - Rocky Wood
3. **'Salem's Lot**
   - Glenn Chadbourne
4. **Under the Dome**
   - Stephen Spignesi
5. **Mr. Mercedes**
   - Bev Vincent
6. **The Stand**
   - Scott Ian, co-founder of Anthrax.
7. **Revival**
8. **Finders Keepers**
   - Bev Vincent
9. **Bazaar of Bad Dream**
10. **Joyland**
    - Dave Hinchberger

11. **Eyes of the Dragon**
12. **Carrie**
    - Carrie Screenwriter - Lawrence Cohen
13. **IT**
    - Additional DJ Art
14. **End of Watch**
    - Bev Vincent
15. **Night Shift**
    - Jack Haringa
16. **Firestarter**
    - Lisa Morton
17. **Different Seasons**
18. **Pet Sematary**
    - Lucy Taylor
19. **Christine**
20. **Cujo**

21. Thru 28 **Dark Tower** – All Eight Covers! - Robin Furth
22. **The Outsider**
23. **Dreamcatcher**
    - Michael Sauers
24. **Thinner**
25. **The Green Mile**
    - David Leslie Johnson
26. **Needful Things**
    - Jeff Strand
27. **Sleeping Beauties**
28. **Elevation**
29. **Bag of Bones**
    - Mick Garris, director.

MORE! Listed at StephenKingCatalog.com

. . . .

You can subscribe to the New King Cover Series!

If you would like to subscribe we will give you a number that is permanently yours for the whole subscription!

See All Covers at StephenKingCatalog.com/Glenn Chadbourne Category

Stephen King Catalog 1987 ~ 2019 The Overlook Connection Bookstore

. . . .

PO Box 1934, Hiram, Georgia 30141 678-567-9777
StephenKingCatalog.com   OverlookConnection.com   overlookcn@aol.com

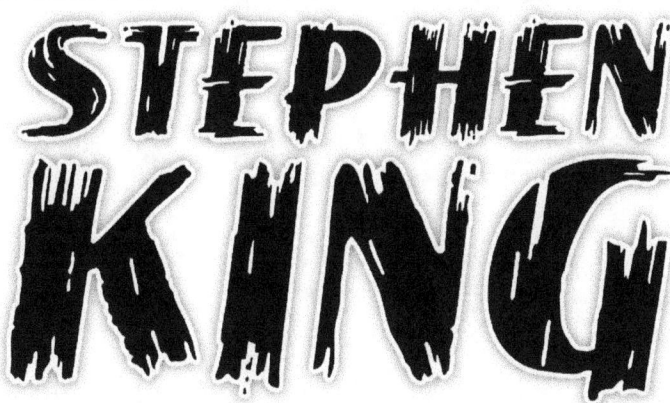

www.ingramcontent.com/pod-product-compliance
Lightning Source LLC
Chambersburg PA
CBHW070947200526
45161CB00001BA/12